THE PUPPY PLACE

GUIDE TO PUPPIES

By Ellen Miles

SCHOLASTIC INC.

No part of this publication may be reproduced, stored in a retrieval system, or transmitted in any form or by any means, electronic, mechanical, photocopying, recording, or otherwise, without written permission of the publisher. For information regarding permission, write to Scholastic Inc., Attention: Permissions Department, 557 Broadway, New York, NY 10012.

ISBN 978-0-545-48433-6

12 11 10 9 8 7 6 5 4 3 2 1   13 14 15 16 17 18/0

Printed in the U.S.A.   40

First printing, January 2013

Book design by Kay Petronio

CONTENTS

INTRODUCTION

A dog wants food and water, a warm corner, fun, exercise, company, loving hands, and someone to look after. A person wants a fun friend, a sweet protector, a kind shoulder to cry on, furry ears to rub, a dear animal who will be a partner in life. What do you need to do to get ready to live with a dog?

The first step is to find each other. The steps after that include getting used to each other: finding the right food and supplies, setting up your house for your new pet, and learning each other's needs. This book was written to help you go through the steps to make a forever home— and a great new life—for a dog or puppy.

SHADOW

"They should have a big house," Lizzie began, "because he needs lots of room to run around."

"Or at least a big yard," said Charles.

"Good!" said Lizzie. "With a fence around it, so he'll be safe."

"I think the family should like to do stuff outdoors," Sammy said. "Because Shadow is going to be an outdoorsy kind of dog. He wouldn't want to be cooped up inside all the time." —Shadow

STEP 1

Planning for a Puppy or Dog

YOU long for a dog of your own, and you know you will take the best possible care of your puppy.

HERE ARE SOME QUESTIONS TO DISCUSS WITH YOUR FAMILY, AND SOME ADVICE ABOUT EACH TOPIC.

What Kind of Dog Do You Want?

- ☐ large dog
- ☐ medium dog
- ☐ small dog
- ☐ long-haired dog
- ☐ short-haired dog
- ☐ show dog
- ☐ working dog
- ☐ athletic dog
- ☐ couch potato
- ☐ service dog
- ☐ purebred dog
- ☐ mutt

☐ ANY KIND OF DOG!

Can you afford dog food and veterinary bills? Get advice from a local animal shelter or veterinarian about costs.

Is anyone allergic to dogs?

If dogs make you cough or sneeze, if they give you asthma or make your eyes water, you could be allergic. If you're not sure, get a doctor's advice before adopting a dog. A doctor, vet, or other expert may be able to recommend a dog that is less likely to cause allergic reactions.

Does everyone get along with dogs?

Consider babies and little children, people who are scared of dogs, or people who dislike them. Dogs are not for everyone.

Can you handle this particular dog?

Like people, dogs' personalities depend on what they're like inside, and what has happened to them. If you have a certain dog in mind, try to learn about this animal and talk about its needs with your family.

What breed is best for your family? Take some time to learn

about the different types of dogs and their needs. A Saint

Bernard might be perfect for an active family that lives in

the country; a Yorkshire terrier may be better for a family

that lives in a city apartment.

Some dogs need to be walked for miles, have to be brushed all the time, or have some other need that could make them hard for a busy family to deal with. And some dogs who have been mistreated may not be able to adjust to a new life, no matter how kind people may be. Before choosing a dog, find out as much as you can from the person you get him from, whether it's a breeder, the owner of the mother dog, someone at the shelter, or the veterinarian.

Even within the same litter, each puppy has his or her own character. Carefully select the pup who is best for you. Another home may be best for the dog you have in mind. Or you may have to make some changes to create a happy home. With love, kindness, and patience, you can help most dogs adjust to the new life you're giving them.

ROCKY

Every night Lizzie studied her "Dog Breeds of the World" poster, and she practically had it memorized. "Bulldogs might look mean and ferocious, but they're not. Stubborn, maybe. But not scary. Most of them are actually sweet little pooches who love to be around people. I hear they can be real clowns, too." —Rocky

Getting Set Up for a New Puppy or Dog

NOW that your family has decided to adopt a dog ...

WHAT EQUIPMENT DO YOU NEED? AND WHAT WILL YOU NEED TO DO? HERE COMES YOUR NEW PUPPY OR DOG! NOW IS THE TIME TO GET READY.

Where Can You Find Your New Pet?

☐ Take in a lost or stray puppy or dog.
☐ Visit a shelter.
☐ Answer an ad to adopt a puppy or dog.
☐ Ask your local veterinarian if he or she knows of a dog who needs a home.
☐ Buy a puppy from a responsible breeder.
☐ Buy a puppy at a pet shop that features pets from animal shelters. *But be careful—pet shops often do a poor job of caring for animals and do not promote responsible breeding. Most pet shops are not good places to find pets.*

Food and Water Dishes

A dog needs his own food and water dishes. Place them in a quiet area, out of the way of other pets and people's feet.

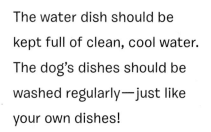

The water dish should be kept full of clean, cool water. The dog's dishes should be washed regularly—just like your own dishes!

Some dogs eat wet food (from cans). Others eat only dry food. Many prefer a combination. Most dogs do best when they eat the same food every day.

Most dogs eat only once a day, in the morning or evening. Some hog all the food down at once, while others graze, eating whenever they feel like it. Puppies need to eat more frequently.

When you take your new pet for a veterinarian visit, ask the vet's advice on the best feeding plan for your new pet.

As for dog biscuits, use them to train your dog or to reward him for good behavior. A dog can become overweight and unhealthy if he eats too many treats.

21

What about other food that dogs get ahold of by themselves? Some dogs will eat anything. If you're concerned about something your dog has eaten, call the vet right away to ask for advice. Spoiled food, chocolate, and certain plants can be especially dangerous to dogs.

GOLDIE

Goldie skidded across the kitchen floor, heading straight for the Bean's plate of French toast.

"Hold on!" said Charles. "That's not puppy food!" He scrambled to get to the plate before Goldie did. —Goldie

Collar and Tags

Every dog needs a collar with tags. Check with your veterinarian about the tags your town requires. Some towns require dog licenses, and others require a tag that says the dog is up-to-date with her rabies shot. Be sure your dog has these tags on her collar at all times. Also, put identification on the dog's collar. Get a tag made with your name and phone number, or write this information on the collar in permanent marker.

You should be able to slip two fingers between the collar and the dog's neck to make sure it's tight enough not to catch on fences and bushes, but loose enough so the pup can breathe easily.

Leash

What kind of leash does your dog need?
The answer depends on where and
how you are walking your dog. If you
walk on a busy sidewalk or another
area where you need to keep your
dog close to you, buy a short
training leash, from
four to six feet long.

If you take your
dog to an open
area that is not
fenced, you might
try a retractable
leash. These let a
dog move fifteen
to twenty-five feet
away from you while
still clipped on.

Poop Bags

In most neighborhoods, the law requires you to clean up after your dog. It's polite and healthy to do this anywhere you walk your dog. Bring along your own supply of bags, unless your area happens to have poop-bag dispensers. Ask a fellow dog owner to show you the clean-hands trick: Wear the plastic bag like a glove while you pick up the poop, then flip the bag inside out while you carry it to a trash can.

What about your own yard? Ask your parents to help you plan how to keep your yard and home clean.

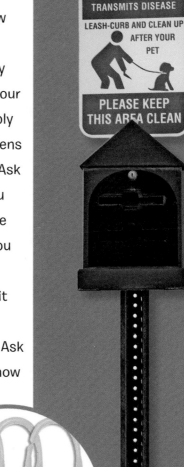

PET WASTE
TRANSMITS DISEASE
LEASH-CURB AND CLEAN UP
AFTER YOUR
PET
PLEASE KEEP
THIS AREA CLEAN

Crate

Many dogs are trained to stay quietly in a crate at certain times of day. This is especially helpful for dogs or puppies who might bark, chew, or cause damage when they are left alone. It's also a useful habit for dogs who need to travel in cars or on planes; they'll feel comfortable and happy in an enclosed space.

Crates also act as dens where dogs can retreat and get quiet time. Crates let you separate your dog from small children, parties, or other situations that work better with the dog out of the room. Some pups learn to go to their crates when they want to be left alone or to sleep.

Sleeping Spot

Even if your dog doesn't need a crate and even if he's allowed to sleep on your bed or couch, he may like having his own special bed in a warm, private spot. You can make a bed from an old pillow or blanket, or find

a dog bed at a pet shop. Consider putting this bed in a corner, under a table, or near your bed. Dogs feel safe and cozy in a place that feels a little like a cave.

Great Crate Tips

 Give your dog a treat in the crate. The dog will learn to see the crate as a good thing.

 Put the crate in a quiet room, but leave the room door open so the dog can hear and smell—if not necessarily see—what's going on.

 Cover the top of the crate with a blanket or towel to make it feel more like a cozy den or cave.

FLASH

Flash wasn't sure exactly what the girl was saying, but he knew it was about him, and he knew it was good. Even though he still missed his own people, he was starting to feel safe with these children. But he was tired of being cooped up! He needed to run.
—Flash

FROM THE PUPPY PLACE

MOOSE

In Moose, the Petersons foster a Great Dane puppy who was kept chained up for the first six months of his life. As a result, Moose is a scaredy-dog, frightened by any new thing: wind, voices, quick movements, everything! Charles works to gently introduce him to new situations. It's important to let go of expectations with a new dog and work with your family to help him adjust to living with you.

STEP 3

Meeting Basic Needs

HERE'S

how to keep your dog in peak

condition from nose to tail.

What Do Dogs Do All Day?

- [ ] sleep
- [ ] eat
- [ ] go for a walk
- [ ] play with another dog or a person
- [ ] look out the window
- [ ] chew on a bone or toy
- [ ] get brushed or petted
- [ ] act as a working dog or service dog

FROM THE PUPPY PLACE

PRINCESS

Lizzie and Charles's aunt Amanda owns a doggy day care called Bowser's Backyard. People bring their dogs, who stay all day, rest, and play with the other dogs, while their owners go to work and school.

Clean and Comfortable

No matter what kind of dog he is, you want to make him as comfortable and confident as possible, as fast as possible. This means feeding him, keeping him clean and warm, and helping him get used to your family's routine.

A new dog may need a bath and/or brushing. Get adult help with this; one person can hold the dog while the other washes or brushes him. Most dogs do not need baths very often, but if a dog is very dirty you might need to bathe him.

For a bath, you can work outside with a hose that has warm water, use the bathtub, or for smaller dogs, line the kitchen sink with a towel.

Use a sprayer to soak the dog, saving the head and face for last. Lather with a small amount of pet soap, using your fingertips to scrub gently down to the dog's skin.

Rinse, and gently dry with a towel. If you can, keep the dog in the tub for a few minutes; she's going to shake off, and suds and water will go flying, so you'll want to let her do this in a place that's easy to clean. Most dogs won't put up with a

hair dryer, so a crate or bathroom with a bath mat may be a good place to drip and dry for a while.

Once your dog is washed, knots and mats in the fur and undercoat will be looser. Brush gently with a wire brush when your dog is mostly dry. For tough cleaning problems or terrible tangles, consider taking your dog to the vet or to a pet groomer.

Cuddling Time

Dogs love to be with their people. Find out how your dog likes to be petted. Does she like her chest or belly rubbed? Maybe he likes having his head scratched, or enjoys long strokes along his back and sides. Spend quiet time cuddling with your dog. Tell her your secrets. This is a great way to bond with your new pet.

Play and Exercise

Dogs need to be walked outside at least three times a day—morning, afternoon or early evening, and before bed. Walk at least long enough for dogs to "do their business," but a longer walk will help keep your dog healthy and happy.

Some people organize playdates with other dogs, hire a dog walker, or take their pets to dog parks or doggy day cares. Play with other dogs is important in helping dogs learn to get along with others. This is called socialization.

Remember, if you take your dog in the car, it is very important to never, ever leave him in the car with the windows up—not even for a few minutes. Even on cool days, heat can build up quickly inside a closed-up car, and a dog can get very sick or even die.

Dogs may go outside alone to dog runs (fenced-in spaces), tie-outs, fenced yards, or yards with invisible fences, but this isn't the best situation for a dog. If your family doesn't have the time to get exercise *with* the dog, it might be best to consider a different kind of pet. Dogs want to be with their people.

PATCHES

"I would never tie Buddy up outside like this." Charles felt so sorry for the lonely little pup. "I think it's mean. Dogs like to be with people, not left alone by themselves."
—Patches

There are lots of ways to play with your dog. You can teach him to retrieve a ball (don't use a stick—they can cause injuries when dogs chew on them), play a game of hide-and-seek, or work on training exercises like *sit* or *heel*. If your dog gets too excited while playing and begins to bark, jump on you, or nip at you, take a "time-out" for some quiet petting.

Housebreaking

When puppies are tiny, some people assign a special pad or stack of newspapers to be the "toilet." Soon puppies are old enough to learn to do their business outside. You can follow this potty procedure for them—or for an older pup who doesn't know what to do.

Attach a leash and walk the puppy to the door. Say, "Want to GO OUT?" Then go outside. When the pup "does her business," praise her. GOOD DOG! Some people use words such as GO POTTY. (Later, these words will cue the dog to go in an unfamiliar place, for example while traveling.)

Praise your pup for going in the right place. With patience, kindness, and praise, she'll get the idea quickly. Pretty soon she'll go to the door when you say, "GO OUT?" And after that she'll go to the door to let you know she needs to go out.

Be willing and available to take your dog out during this learning time. If you're slow or if you don't go out when the dog cues you (by barking, whining, sniffing the floor, or circling), he'll get confused and have trouble

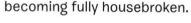

becoming fully housebroken.

Never yell at or hit your dog for making a mistake. And whatever you do, don't rub his nose in his mistakes. That won't help at all. Instead, be gentle and patient. Ask yourself whether you are taking him out often enough. In time, he won't need so many trips outside.

SWEETIE

STEP 4

Very Basic Training

THE best advice I've ever heard comes from a friend who has had dogs all her life: "Just love him." Start by believing that your dog is a good dog, and telling him so as often as you can.

Not only is this a loving attitude to take toward your dog, but it's good dog psychology. Trainers call it positive reinforcement, and they find that it is the most effective way to train dogs. Praise, pet, and treat your dog when she does something good, and ignore or gently stop the

dog when she does something you don't want her to do.
To ignore your dog: cross your arms across your chest and
look away. Stand very still until the dog stops doing the
"naughty" thing. When she stops, praise her and go on with
whatever you were doing. This works well with dogs who
bark for attention or who like to jump up on people or nip
at their hands.

It's also a good idea to make it easy for the dog to behave well. For example, if you have a puppy who likes to chew, don't leave your shoes around. Better yet, keep her in a crate when nobody is watching her, or penned in one room, like the kitchen or a bathroom, where she can't get into things. Make sure the garbage and dog food are out of reach, and give her a special toy that will keep her busy.

Obedience class or a trainer can get your dog on the right track. Puppy kindergarten is a great place for puppies to learn and to get socialized at the same time. And trainers can help with common problems like jumping up, barking, or chewing. Here are a few pointers for starters. When you are training your dog, begin with short sessions. Most puppies and some dogs have a hard time concentrating for more than ten minutes at a time.

First, teach your dog to sit for a treat. Say SIT. Hold the treat above his head, and he might automatically sit. If he doesn't, gently push his rear into a sitting position while saying SIT. Say GOOD DOG! and give him the treat. Soon he'll realize that holding your hand above his head means to sit. Pretty soon you won't need the treat—just the first signal or word—to get him to sit. GOOD DOG.

When your dog is doing something you don't like, don't meet his eyes. Stop him, hold him, and say STOP to get him to quit doing something.

Another tip: Don't use your dog's name in place of STOP! If you do, he might learn that his name has a bad message and he won't come when you call. Use his name when he's being good, and soon you'll have no trouble getting him to come to you with a big doggy smile on his face.

In time, you'll need to teach your dog other commands, as well. Dogs should know DOWN, in which they stop and lie down. This is a great emergency command, in case your dog gets loose or is chasing a car or doing some other action you want to stop. DROP IT or LEAVE IT is helpful, too, for when dogs pick up things they shouldn't eat. Dogs should also know STAY, which helps them to understand your expectations when you leave the house or walk away from them. Many owners teach their dogs HEEL to get them to walk in the right position while on a leash. A trainer can advise you on other commands your dog should know.

Once your dog knows his basic commands, you can have fun teaching him tricks. Here's one that's easy to teach: You can train your dog to roll over and show his stomach with a short command such as DEAD DOG or BANG or FLOP. Say the word while gently pushing the dog to the floor, rolling him over, and rubbing his belly. Since a belly rub is a reward to him, he'll quickly learn to roll over when you say the magic word.

The key to training is to show the dog what to do and to reward him for doing it. What's more, it's easier for a dog to be good when his needs are met. Make sure your dog gets plenty of exercise, play, and fresh air. Many dog owners say, "A tired dog is a good dog."

Cody had run completely out of steam and was lying curled up on the red rug by the sink, snoozing. His big paws, with their velvety-soft pink pads, twitched as if he were still running around the kitchen in his dreams. "Awww!" said Lizzie. —Cody

STEP 5

Vet Check

EVERY

pet needs a vet!

Things to Talk to the Vet About:

- [ ] vaccination shots
- [ ] fleas, ticks, and heartworm
- [ ] tags and licenses
- [ ] health checkup
- [ ] spaying or neutering
- [ ] getting a microchip
- [ ] trimming claws
- [ ] training
- [ ] planning emergency care

FROM THE PUPPY PLACE

PUGSLEY

The Peterson family takes every foster pet to see Dr. Gibson. The cost of veterinarian visits is an important thing to consider before getting a dog.

First, it's good to know that your pet is healthy, getting enough to eat (but not too much), and growing well.

The vet can check your dog for worms, ticks, and fleas. You should be sure this is done before bringing a new dog into your house.

The vet can also tell you what shots your dog needs to keep from getting sick. He can schedule shots and spaying or neutering for puppies, who must reach a certain age before they are "fixed" so they can't have puppies of their own. And he can give you advice on daily care and any problems you might have with your new pup.

There are two other important things your vet can do for your pet: prevent loss and plan for emergencies. A vet can place a tiny microchip in your dog's body during a quick operation in the office. The microchip holds information about you so that if someone finds your dog, they can let you know. It also sends out a radio signal so that you can find your dog yourself.

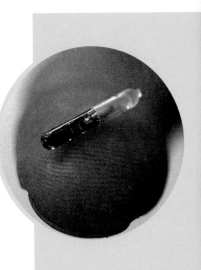

A vet can also help you put together a plan for emergency medical care for your dog: whom to call or where to go if your dog is hurt or gets sick when the vet isn't available to help.

PATCHES

It was safe to let Buddy and Patches play together, because Charles knew Buddy had been to the vet recently and all his shots were up to date. That would protect him and Patches from passing around any bad germs.
—Patches

STEP 6

Fun, Love, and Understanding

THIS could be your dog's favorite chapter!

Dog Body Language:

Rolling on the Back: friendliness; "You're the boss!"

Tail Wagging: friendliness or interest; "Hi!"

Licking: trying to get attention in a friendly, bossy way

Meeting Your Eyes: listening, watching, and usually willing

Not Meeting Your Eyes: worried, or unwilling to do what you ask

Panting, Pacing Around: hot, stressed out, or sick

Yawning: wants to please you, but not willing to do what you want

How to Speak Dog

Sniffing: "Who are you?" (When dogs meet, they sniff each other's rears.)

Sneezing: Some people say that when a dog sneezes, he's laughing.

Bowing (stretching the front legs out): "Want to play?"

Barking: Different barks can mean greetings, warnings, fun, or worry.

Ears Laid Back: can show fear or dislike, but in some dogs this is a greeting

Growling or Snarling: warning or threatening

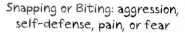

Snapping or Biting: aggression, self-defense, pain, or fear

Dog Fun

- [ ] squeaky toy
- [ ] tug-of-war rope
- [ ] fleece toy
- [ ] rawhide bone
- [ ] marrow bone
- [ ] Kong toy (stuffed with cheese or peanut butter)
- [ ] puzzle ball (with treat inside)

Scientists say that people who have dogs are often healthier than those who don't. For example, some studies say that kids who grow up with furry pets have less asthma and fewer allergies. People with dogs were found to have fewer heart attacks and better heart health than people without dogs. Experts say that dogs help their owners feel happier and calmer, as well.

Children who are responsible for a dog may even do better in school. Kids who care for pets learn to understand what someone else needs, and to put their pet's needs first. Here's wishing you health and happiness with your forever pup.

BUDDY

Buddy looked from one happy face to the other. What was everybody so excited about? He had known it all along. He belonged here in this house, with this family. Buddy had found the perfect forever home.
—Buddy

CHEWY and CHICA

LOST

Have you seen Zeno?

Just In Case

Reward if found.
He has dog tags with name and address.
Please call if you find him: 123-1234

SAD things can happen
to the best dogs.

Lost Puppy!

Experts say that "lost" dogs will often keep moving, getting more and more lost. When looking for a missing dog, look farther than the last place the dog was seen. Put up posters showing a photograph of your pet. Let your local animal control officer, police station, and vet know that your dog is missing. Get the word out through a local online news site or town Facebook page—anywhere someone who found a dog would look.

Best of all, have your dog microchipped [see page 58]. This lets your vet help you track your dog, and can provide your contact information to whoever finds him.

ZIGGY

Charles stuck a hand into his pocket and pulled out a hot dog. He took a few silent steps closer to Ziggy, then sat down on the ground. He knew just what to do now. He broke off a piece of hot dog and tossed it gently in Ziggy's direction. . . . He threw another piece, and another, and Ziggy found them and chomped them. In another minute, Ziggy was almost close enough to touch. —Ziggy

If Your Pet Dies

Even with the most loving care, bad things can happen.
Dogs or puppies can get sick or hurt and not get better.
When you own a dog or puppy, focus on giving him the best
life possible. Then, if something happens, you will know
that your pet was happy. It's a sad fact of life that dogs and
other animals don't live as long as people. And sometimes
kids have to go through the death of a pet.

Lots of people hold and touch their pets after they die.
This helps them to say good-bye. Pets can be buried in your
yard, or a vet can have them cremated so you can bury or
keep the ashes. You can make or buy a gravestone or other
memorial.

After your pet dies, share photographs and stories with your family, and treasure your memories together. After a while, you may be ready to open your heart and home to a new pet.

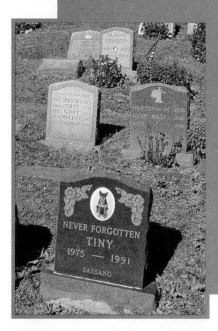

breeder: someone who pairs strong, healthy dogs in order to get the strongest, healthiest pups

breed: a particular kind of plant or animal; to mate and give birth to young

crate: a cage or container for a pet

groomer: a professional who washes, trims, and brushes pets

housebreaking: teaching a dog the right place for toilet activities

litter: a number of baby animals that are born at the same time to the same mother

neuter: to make a male animal unable to produce young

positive reinforcement: using praise and rewards to teach your pet good behavior

shelter: a place where an animal that is not wanted can stay

socialization: helping a dog learn to get along with people, other dogs, and other pets

spay: to make a female animal unable to produce young

stray: a cat or dog that has wandered away from home or that has no home

veterinarian: a doctor who is trained to diagnose and treat sick or injured animals

working dog: breed developed to do work such as guarding, hunting, or herding

WEBSITES

This book is just a start. There's always more to learn about dogs! Check out these websites, and don't forget that your library probably has lots of books about dogs and dog care.

The American Society for the Prevention of Cruelty to Animals (ASPCA): Dog Care:
aspca.org/Pet-care/dog-care

Eukanuba Puppy Guide:
eukanuba.com/en-US/puppy-guide/top-10-puppy-care-tips.jspx

Hill's Pet Nutrition: Puppy Care:
hillspet.com/dog-care/puppy-care.html

IAMS Top Ten Puppy Care Tips:
iams.com/pet-health/dog-article/top-10-puppy-care-tips Petco Care Sheets: Your New Puppy:
petco.com/Content/ArticleList/Article/32/1/2561/Your-New-Puppy.aspx

Purina: About Puppy Care:
purina.com/dog/puppy-care/puppycare.aspx

WebMD for Pets: Healthy Dogs:
pets.webmd.com/dogs/guide/puppy-care

INDEX

PHOTO CREDITS